Brothel

Stephanie M. Wytovich

Brothel © 2016 by Stephanie M. Wytovich

Published by Raw Dog Screaming Press
Bowie, MD

All rights reserved.

First Edition

Cover illustration: Steven Archer
Book design: M. Garrow Bourke

ISBN: 978-1-935738-83-1
Library of Congress Control Number: 2016940275

Printed in the United States of America

www.RawDogScreaming.com

Table of Contents

Absinthe 13
Action Shot 14
Adult Play 15
Amoral 16
Appetite 17
Automatic Woman 18
Besotted 19
Bewitched 20
Blind Obedience 21
Branded 22
Brothel 23
Burlesque 24
Calling off Work 25
Candy 26
Carnal Charisma 27
Casanova 28
Champagne After Midnight 29
Cherry Blossom 30
Clitorial 31
Courtship 32
Dance 33
Debauchery 34
Deeper 35
Deep Throat 36
Die-sect 37
Dirty Sheets 38
Drink, Drank, Drunk 39
Drink Up, Lie Down 40
Dysmorphic 41

Eat Me 42

Ecstasy 43

Erotic Asphyxiation 44

Eve 45

Evening Girl 46

Evidence 47

Exit 55, Cincinnati, Columbus 48

Fake It Until You Make It 49

Flesh Notes 50

Flirtation 51

Foursome 52

French 53

From Behind 54

G-Spot 55

Gasp for Air 56

Girlfriend Experience 57

Graphic Display of Affection 58

Grass Stains 59

Gratification, Scarification 60

Gravitation 61

Hardcore 62

Harlot 63

He Asked Me to Stay 64

Hedonist 65

Heroin Chic 66

Hotel Room 67

Hunger 68

I Cover the Wall's Mouth 69

Indiscreet 70

Infidelity 71

Infiltrate From Within 72

Intimacy 73

Jilted	74
Job Title	75
Joint Custody	76
Juice	77
Just Because	78
Justifiable	79
Kama Sutra	80
Keeping Tabs	81
Killing Strangers	82
Kinky as a Definition of Him	83
Kitten	84
Lady Killer	85
Leaving Him for Dead	86
Lewd Behavior	87
Lonely Soul	88
Love Scars	89
Lust Is My Deadly Sin	90
Madness	91
Man-eater	92
Masturbation	93
May I?	94
Ménage a trois	95
Miscarriage	96
Miss Behave	97
Naked	98
Natural Born Sinner	99
Never and Me	100
New Orleans	101
Nobody's Whore	102
Nymphomaniac	103
Obedience	104
Obituary	105

One-Night Stand 106
Open for Business, Closed for Love 107
Orgasm 108
Out of Service Sign 109
Peepshow 110
Penance 111
Perversion 112
Photograph 113
Pillow Fight 114
Purge 115
Queen of Hearts 116
Queer 117
Quickie 118
Quiet, They're on to Us 119
Quitting Time 120
Remember Not to Cry 121
Replacement 122
Resilient 123
Ripped Stockings 124
Rough Play 125
Route 70 at Midnight 126
Sadism 127
Secret Lovers 128
Sexual Scars 129
Shameless Sex 130
Slippery When Wet 131
Stripped 132
Symmetry 133
The Shed 134
Tied and Taken 136
Tipsy, Tanked, Trashed 137
Transaction 138

Trust Me	139
The Flavor	140
Ugly Little Moment	141
Unanimous	142
Untamed	143
Untie Me	144
Used	145
Vaginal Roses	146
Velvet Underground	147
Vibrate	148
Vicious Girls	149
Violent Fantasies	151
Viper Bite	152
Waltz	153
Watching Him	154
Weaning Myself Off	155
Welcome	156
Whipping Post	157
White Dahlia Abortion	158
Wordplay	160
X-rated	161
Xenophile	162
Yawn	163
Yell for Help	164
Yellow Dress	165
Yes-Girl	166
You, Always You	167
YouTerUs	168
Zelophilia	169

Advance Praise for Brothel

"*Brothel* comes to you like a lover in the dark; the movements initially hesitant, but with growing confidence and passion as it pulls you in deeper. Before you know it, the poetry—Wytovich's words and rhythms—are in your head, your heart, and your gut, moving all three in a way that you haven't felt since your first time, lo, those many years ago. Don't. Miss. This." —Paul Michael Anderson, Editor of *Jamais Vu* and author of *Bones are Made to be Broken*

"Stephanie M. Wytovich's new poetry collection is a triumph of prismatic storytelling. The poems in *Brothel* have multiple shades and angles, and each one's a window into a secret world I longed to explore—in spite of the bloodstains, and sometimes because of them. It was an animated read for me. As the characters twisted themselves in and out of deadly pleasure, I shivered in delight and shuddered in sad fascination. I feared these girls, but I also wanted to fight, fuck, and be these girls. This is a beautiful collection, and it's safe to assume I'll be a frequent visitor to Stephanie's *Brothel* for years to come." —Jessica McHugh, author of *The Green Kangaroos*

"Wielding words with lyrical precision, Stephanie Wytovich has crafted a dangerous, dark, and oh-so-very-beautiful journey in *Brothel*. Filled with the raw heat and obsessive passions of love, this collection immerses the reader in the delicious miasma of humanity; at once depraved and holy, Brothel is poetry as weapon, as caress, as submission. Absolutely glorious." —Peter Adam Solomon, Bram Stoker Award-nominated author of *All Those Broken Angels*

"I didn't quite know what I was in for when I slipped into Stephanie M. Wytovich's *Brothel*. Now here I stand on the sidewalk outside, shielding my eyes against the harsh light of day. My hair is a mess, my mascara smudged, and I'm inexplicably missing a shoe. After *Brothel* I'll never be clean again. …or feel as satisfied as I am now." —Kristin Dearborn, *Stolen Away* and *Woman in White*

Author's Note:

Welcome to my brothel.
Come, stay, make yourself at home.
I cater to any and all types here.

Now tell me, what do you prefer? Women? Men? Both?
What turns you on? What gets you off?
My girls are talented, trained by myself and my colleague here, and we spared no expense teaching them the art of making love.

Oh! But how rude of me! Let me introduce my right hand.
Ladies. Gentleman. I give you Madam XXX.

The Madam and I met a year ago under less than savory circumstances at a rest stop in Ohio. I was half-asleep in the back of my car, looking for a new muse, looking for something or someone to take me to places and put me in situations that I hadn't experienced before, and when she showed up on the side of the road in a red dress with a knife in her hands, I knew we were in for an adventure. Together, we studied pleasure, mastered pain. She showed me what Heaven could be, and I showed her what Hell was. We were the perfect combination of sadism and masochism.

And we never needed a safe word.

So sit back, relax, and let me tell you some stories. Some stories about sex, about hate, about pleasure and pain. Let me show you how fucking can kill you and bring you back, how a good night in bed can break you and put you back together again. If there's anything that scares me in this world, it's sacrificing a part of myself for another person, but if working with The Madam has taught me anything, it's that there are some holes that can't be filled, and others…well, others that can just be filled over and over again.

—Stephanie M. Wytovich

Dedication

For Lust, For Love.
You evil, beautiful sins.
It was a wild ride.

"When play dies it becomes the Game. When sex dies it becomes Climax. All games contain the idea of death."
—Jim Morrison, *The Lords and the New Creatures*

Absinthe

Green is my favorite color
I like the way it spins, turns,
lifts me up and lets me fly higher
than I ever have before;
it's electric, and like a Jim Morrison song
it lights my fire
lights me aflame
lets me burn throughout the night;
I drink green to reach
hypnotic trance
to be alert,
wise to everything
and everyone
around me
who's real
and
riding
the
same
storm.

Action Shot

The Johns want us to take it,
take it like we owe it to them,
like we deserve it,
like we want it,
but we are not whores,
not their substitute wives
and we instigate the action
just like we call the shots;
it's just a matter of deciding whether
we'll use our cunts to please them,
or the barrel of a gun.

Adult Play

When it comes to getting me off
I don't need any foreplay;
no candles, no wax—
you can keep your toys
and your dirty words;
I'll take care of myself as you watch me
give myself the
five-finger discount
so I can keep
my pride.

Amoral

There's right and there's wrong
just like the kind of woman you'd marry
and the kind you'd just fuck;
but my morals are whiskey
my lips a soft rain
and I like to drink and stay wet
mix my pleasure
with my pain

Appetite

It's simple satisfaction—
a quick meal to stave off the hunger;
she sets the bed for dinner
the same time every night,
and I come home to her
and eat like the glutton
I am

Automatic Woman

Turn the lights off,
Turn my body on—
In, out. In out.
It's routine.
It's work.
And I don't
have to wait
until Friday
to get
paid.

Besotted

There's something about the way
you play all that jazz,
something about the way the notes
slide off your instrument and run down my body,
settle between my legs
it makes me want to take my clothes off,
makes me want to dance,
dance between sheets
between bodies
and I vibrate as I
sip bourbon from the bottle
tell you all my secrets
tell you about the skeletons in my closet
and the bodies in my bed
and it feels okay because
I know you're not really listening,
not with your gaze glued to my chest,
so I'll be honest, I'll confess,
I'll let the Devil hear my sins.

Bewitched

Butterfly kisses
Twisted tongues
She'll wrap you around her finger
Poke spells into your lungs

Blind Obedience

You're still and you're blindfolded
arms bound with my satin sheets
and I need you to be quiet,
but I want you to beg;

Now shhhh…
and listen to me close,
I'm going to have you now
and I need you to do
exactly what I say, when I say
now kiss me,
kiss me and tell me
you love me,
then get on all fours,
and let me hear you
scream.

Branded

At first, I didn't think anything of it; lots of guys made me promise to be their girl, but it was all just an act, just a game we'd play to get each other off and pretend that for a few hours we weren't as lonely as we were. But then there was one, one John who was serious, too serious, and he said I wasn't allowed to be with any other men, and I told him that it was part of my job, part of why he was with me in the first place, and he laughed, laughed in this manic kind of way as he took out his knife and placed it in the fireplace, placed it against my thigh. I cried then, cried for the first time that night, the second was after he was gone, after the insignia started to cool, started to heal in a bloody NW. He'd post-marked me for newlywed; his bridal whore, his branded girl for life. And now nobody plays with me anymore.

Brothel

There's a brothel in my hand
and it's open for business, providing me with pleasure
while I pay it with my pain; I close my eyes and see,
see for the first time as immeasurable desires wake
inside me, screaming, panting: legs spread apart,
arms open wide, lips pursed, parted. The women are my
invitations, the men my RSVPs, and I'll accept their summons
to come, to stay, to eat and drink the fruits and juices of the sweet gardens
in front of me—pulsing, dripping, rich with
honey, sweet with wine.

My mouth is open and I'm ready to inhale,
ready to swallow, and they've promised
they'd fill me, that they'd keep me nice and full;
I slip my fingers through the front door and
I'm met with a warm hello,
as I'm taken inside—as I'm taken—and I
think I'll stay here for a while, locked inside
my brothel where the animals like to breed.

Burlesque

Piece by piece,
I take it all off: slowly, carefully. My clothes
touch the floor, my body the stage. In their eyes,
I'm a goddess, a star, and this foreplay, this seduction
is important, my favorite part of the act,
and I'll admit I like to tease, like to taunt
especially when I have no intention
of ever following through.

Calling off Work

She woke up with him inside her,
his blue eyes, ice, against the sun; he was soft,
gentle, and they made love until her alarm went off,
and then fucked for two hours after.

Candy

Sweet on my tongue
warm in my mouth
I eat her every day
for my sugar high
at noon.

Carnal Charisma

Take a lover who looks at you as if you're his world,
as if he'd storm armies in order to stand next to you,
drown the sky in order to drink from your lips;
this lover will be one who whispers instead of screams,
who gives instead of begs, and when he leaves,
he'll leave the door open so you can leave with him,
and that way none of this seems hurtful, in fact, sometimes
it even seems like love.

Casanova

He comes to see me every Thursday night; we've never had sex, but he likes to watch me work. He even brings me flowers—two tulips—before I clock in. He kisses me on the cheek, runs his hand down my neck, and then he sits in the corner of the room while I climb atop my client. No one knows he's there but me, and when I'm done, he takes me into the washroom and bathes me till I'm clean. He dries me off with the towel he's brought, and then dresses me in satin, tucks me into bed. Before he leaves, he recites a poem, a poem about obedience, and I hate him, hate him so much, but he pays me well, well and on time, and tulips are my favorite flower.

Champagne After Midnight

Lights off, candle wax down your back
I cover you in flames, but face down, you don't scream,
you let me straddle you,
the black silk of my lingerie against your thighs,
I kiss your neck, kiss your spine,
tongue the spot behind your ears, but you can't see me,
can't see the pink blush that moistens in-between my legs.
and there's a bottle on the table,
an empty glass with the imprint of your lips
and when you whisper, I bite my tongue
fight the urge to come,
but you turn around and grab my hips,
trace circles around my breasts
and when you're inside me,
I taste champagne,
and when you're done
I swallow midnight.

Cherry Blossom

The girls called me Cherry because I'd blossom
pink and red, because I'd bloom the moment I'd enter a room,
but the boys, they called me Flower, and I was an easy little bud;
it didn't take much to ruffle my petals, and when we'd pollinate,
they'd say I tasted like honey, that I was sticky and sweet,
that I smelled like Spring when I came.

Clitorial

Before I started working here, here in this Brothel that's very much my home, here for Madam XXX, who's very much my mom, I had to audition, pass a series of tests. There were girls and there were boys, there were women and there were men, and I often wondered what it was that they saw in me, what it was about my tongue, or my hands, my smile or my eyes that brought them to climax, that gave them a few moments of peace. They'd come around at night and mom would give them my room number, and I'd practice and I'd practice, because that's how talents are made, how clients are made, and now I get to come and go as I please, taking numbers, taking cash, and mom treats me like one of her own; she even kisses me goodnight before I fall asleep.

Courtship

Sex is simple if I keep it that way, if I don't get to know them, if I keep my feelings hidden, keep them locked away inside. It's dangerous to get to know my partners, to move beyond this touch and that, and I'll show them my body but never my heart, never my soul, and that way the pain that's associated with love can never touch me; I'm immune. Safe. Protected. I'll court their desires, date their pleasures, but when you've lived as I've lived, worked as I've worked, the power of sex has to remain with me. I can only be their lover. Never their love.

Dance

I remember the first man I danced for,
but I don't remember dancing and I think that has
something to do with the absinthe, with the way we shot
down green fairies from the sky and placed them on our tongues,
the way we let them burn, caramelized and pure, as we kissed each other's fingertips
watched the world start to vibrate, start to glow.

Debauchery

Every day is Saturday night when you're living on drugs and booze, spiraling with pills, joyriding on the trance; I almost forget what it's like to be sober, what it feels like not to be high, but the adrenaline running through my veins makes me happy, makes me scream, and I can't picture anything more perfect than your body pressed against mine while the tablet dissolves on our tongues.

Deeper

Soft touches, careful caresses,
get these men away from me; I've been around too long
to believe there's anything gentle about sex, so push harder,
get deeper, I want to feel you inside, growing, expanding; I want you to dominate
me, to take me, to make me forget that fucking is supposed to be about love when
we both known it's all about pain.

Deep Throat

I shoved my pride down my throat,
swallowed my past, shut my eyes;
it hurt to breathe with all that death in my lungs,
with all that cemented regret,
those unfelt feelings that I kept disregarding,
kept running past,
and the taste of him still sits on my tongue,
souring my memories
with murder and sex
and I wonder if I'll digest it all soon,
if I'll break down his heart with anger and acid,
let him dissolve inside my corpse,
my body,
his coffin.

Die-sect

Lay down,
get comfortable,
I'll make you feel things you've never felt before
but just ignore the blood;
it's a formality more than anything
and I promise you,
after a few minutes,
you'll feel nothing at all.

Dirty Sheets

There's blood on my bed
from the tears that I've cried,
every time you took me,
every time I died.

Drink, Drank, Drunk

I hated myself a little bit more every day, but I saw no other way out of this; everything became too much, and when it became too much, I broke, broke harder and into more pieces than I ever had before. I'd try to collect them, scavenge and scour what I could, but there were absences and empty places that I couldn't fill, and when I couldn't fill them, I stopped being able to feel. So I took drugs and I drank. Sometimes I whored around to try and dull the pain, but it never worked. So I took more drugs, drank more booze, had more sex. When it came down to it, I was self-destructive, a hopeless romantic. I'd kill myself every day if it meant I'd see his face again. Even if only in my memory, in my drunk and my high. This death was sweet, poison, and bitter, and I'd shoot it every day.

Drink Up, Lie Down

I told myself that I'm going to quit drinking, that I'm going to hand in my sinner's card, put away my opium pipe and throw out my weed, but then I sit there, thinking, remembering, recounting those nights, reliving those memories when I laughed without care, when I loved without reason, when I ran down streets, barefoot and happy, dancing to the sound of jazz, when I rode in the back of pickup trucks with the wind against my face screaming at the top of my lungs because I could, because I wanted to, it's those moments with those people that make me pick up my drink, that make me refill my pipe, because in those bars, in those alleys, in those towns, I wasn't some anonymous face, some Jane Doe in a skirt, I was their girl and we drank and fucked and snorted lines off the bar, ran hotel tabs that we couldn't pay, and it was beautiful and we were alive, drunk off each other's body, high off the scent of sex and cocaine.

Dysmorphic

I am a figment of your imagination
I do not exist
I am what you perceive me to be
Beautiful
Willing
Able

But I am not real
I am a shadow of a person
An idea that you've married yourself to
Someone attractive
Healthy
Intelligent

Yet I am neither nor any of those things
I am a whisper, a mirage
The vibration in your peripheral view
And if I turn too fast
I'll disappear,
I'll escape
Once
And
For
All

Eat Me

Circles.
Lines.
Whatever he did with this tongue,
he could have done it forever;
and just the thought of his fingers,
of his lips pressed against my cunt,
makes me bite my lip,
makes me *have to come.*

Ecstasy

He slipped the stamp on my tongue as he kissed me, told me to breathe and close my eyes; he kept asking if I trusted him, but my body felt like wine, loose and ripe, and all I could do was moan as the room began to highlight itself and spin. His hands were on my waist, his tongue in my mouth, and I was floating, floating above the bed, and we made love in the air.

Erotic Asphyxiation

What people don't understand about sex,
is that it's not about love; it's about power,
and when I have the power, then it becomes about
trust. How much do you trust me? Will you let me
wrap my hands around your throat, tie a belt around your neck?
Is there a part of you that wonders what it's like to be breathless,
because there's a part of me that wants to see how you look, wide-eyed
and struggling, your life and orgasm twisting and turning in the
palm of my hand. They say the threat of death is a powerful aphrodisiac, but you know
what they say about curiosity. It killed the cat.

Eve

Call me Eve,
most men do,
but know that a bite of my fruit
comes with a price.

Evening Girl

The job is simple.
I do what I'm told,
and I have to pretend that I like it,
but let me tell you a secret: I don't.
Every orgasm you think you've given me,
I've faked it, faked it once, faked it twice
and part of me actually thinks it's sad that
you get off to my rehearsed moans and my practiced sighs. Remember,
sweetheart, you're not my knight in shining armor, you're a client and
I'm clocked in and working the second you take off my clothes;
and while you may think I'm just a whore,
honey, you're just a paycheck,
and you're the one who's getting fucked.

Evidence

If I wanted to see him again, I knew I had to sin, knew I had to get down on my knees, teach him a thing or two about prayer while I pretended to learn how to confess. I knew he'd give me penance, make me work for my redemption, so I'd be his Catholic school girl, his innocent little toy, let him be the big, bad Devil, the first one to take a bite out of my apple even though we both knew it had been bit and sucked many times before. Like Lazarus, I'd keep coming, keep coming back for more, and I'd leave a trail of bite marks and bruises behind, little love notes written in his flesh. That way he'd have something to remember me by, something to look at in the morning when he recounted his own sins.

Exit 55, Cincinnati, Columbus

I spent my paycheck on a rental car
and slept at every rest stop from Pittsburgh to Cincinnati;
I knew the highways of Ohio by heart
and my insomnia has walked me through gas stations,
pulled me down side roads,
and closed my eyes in motel parking lots
where I sometimes wondered if I'd even wake up.

I wasn't supposed to smoke in the car,
but I hadn't drank in months, and the whiskey song
of the gypsy road called to me like a drunk siren at every bar
I passed. My eyes, tired, dark, soulless—I think you once said—
were too proud to admit they were lost,
that they hadn't seen this place, this face, that exit, that bypass,
so I'd wander the states, crossing borders, doing lines,
hit the cruise control while I chugged Red Bulls,
smoke cigarettes till my mouth went dry.

I'd roll my window down, let the night air slap my face,
and my hair would writhe like copper snakes, a medusa cameo in black
summer knots. I'd nod, I'd dip, I'd fade in and out, sing songs
I didn't know the words to and sometimes I'd scream,
other times I'd cry, but the roads always got longer,
and you always got further away.

Fake It Until You Make It

Plans
yeah, I used to have 'em
I was gonna do big things, you know, see the world, fall in love
but I found myself turnin' tricks too young,
and then things got comfortable and I never left this place
but in some ways,
I guess you could say I became famous
I mean, after all, everyone in this town knows my name
and the fortune, yeah, I got that, too
I just didn't do it as the girl I thought I would
I did it as someone else
someone whose name I took from a cheap romance novel
whose life I made up in my head
and sometimes I miss that girl who I thought I was gonna be,
but she's gone
and I need to make peace with the broad who took her place
cause she ain't goin' nowhere

Flesh Notes

I wrote poetry to his sighs,
to the way he fell asleep,
to the way we'd hold each other so tight as if we were afraid that the other would
disappear if we took a chance and let go;
I wrote love notes to his orgasms,
to the way he'd shake and tremble, hold my hair as he came,
and I'd whisper them in novels, read to him as he fell asleep, asleep in my arms,
and then I'd write him songs,
songs about peace, about sweetness, and security,
and I'd sing them to his dreams,
dreams that I hoped were about me,
and if they weren't, that they were about
something, or someone who made him happy,
something, or someone who made him feel safe.

Flirtation

Her favorite part of the game was initiating it; like a spider,
she lured them in, bathed in silk as she lay in wait and dreamed
about the moment when they'd be beneath her. She'd fantasize
about the second when she could bite and lick and suck and feed,
when she could unravel from her web, stretch her legs, and run,
run, run. It was a careful technique that was passed down from
madam to madam and she was practiced,
a well-trained black widow, and she counted her Johns
like she counted her bills: one at a time.

Foursome

When I woke up, I was covered in bodies that were slick with sweat, wet with blood. There were handprints on my chest, and someone's head between my thighs, and I wanted to run but I was afraid, afraid to move, afraid to see what waited for me on the other side of the door. So I stayed there, wrapped in sheets of crimson, eyes shut, mind racing. I couldn't remember anything, but that wasn't what frightened me; I often blacked out in moments of passion. What scared me was that I'd already hidden the memory from myself, not to mention the weapon, and I was a sneaky broad when it came to murder: I liked to stage my own scenes, solve my own crimes.

French

I didn't have to go to Paris to learn the language of love;
All I had to do was open the house,
and let my clients give me an oral exam.

From Behind

He likes to take me from behind,
my ass in the air,
my back arched
his hands around my throat;
sometimes he'll pull my hair,
kiss my neck, my spine,
and when we come,
it's always together,
ever in sync
mind
and body,
sex
and
soul.

G-Spot

Lay me down, prop me up
it's a journey of show and tell;
my screams will navigate as we touch and play,
despite neither of us knowing where to go;
and if you stay with me,
wet lips, hard flesh, all we ever were
the scent, the descent, the dark and the light
makes the confusion, the exploration of bodies,
an erotic compilation of untapped foreplay
that repeats in our heads
over and over again
as we touch,
as we play
as we scream and laugh
and fuck.

Gasp for Air

Breathe in
breathe out
try not to die,
try not to swallow the plastic around your head,
to not taste the white that's suctioned itself
to your lips, your teeth, your cheeks;
it's getting harder isn't it—I can tell from the bulge in your pants,
but you're getting older
and you've smoked for too long
and one of these days I'm going to laugh
laugh while your lungs cramp,
while they shrivel in your chest,
so please,
smoke another cigarette,
take another puff,
one of these days you're going to murder yourself with sex
and I'm going to be happy to help you do it.

Girlfriend Experience

I'll take you upstairs,
I'll whisper your name
because *"you're the only one, baby"*
is my most-practiced lie,
my hotel-room mantra
and I can promise you that I'm honest,
that I'm an innocent little girl,
but my job is to pretend,
so I'm your virgin prostitute, darling;
now teach me how to sin.

Graphic Display of Affection

He was there and I was there
and together we were in the moment,
the moment that called for something more,
something extra, and I thought he could handle it,
thought he could play, but some men don't know
how to take a knife, and some men take it all too well.

Grass Stains

He dared her
and the whiskey said yes,
and she said yes to the whiskey
and now every time they have sex
she smells fresh-cut grass
knowing her virginity is buried
somewhere in his neighbor's backyard.

Gratification, Scarification

I took off my shirt and slid onto his lap
Get inside me
He kissed me soft, bit my lip and pulled
Make me bleed
He smiled and took out the knife,
    grabbed the back of my neck, licked my throat
    "beg for it"
I gasped, pleaded with my eyes, my dark fuck-me-eyes
and he cut my black bra down the front,
threw it against the wall—
    the blade inched across my chest
    spilled my rubies while I came hard
    against his thigh.
Back arched, tits out, I laughed
Mark me, brand me, make me yours
He slid two fingers in my mouth
Made me show him how I suck
"you already know you're mine—
but I'll make sure you never forget."

Gravitation

I couldn't have stopped if I wanted to,
something was projecting me forward, planning my moves
writing my script, and my body was no longer my own,
it was his, and I was his, and that was the only part of the story
that mattered

Hardcore

Beaten black and blue, the girls told me this was occasionally part of the job, that some Johns got off on the violence and that I'd better find a way to deal with it if I wanted to maintain clientele. I bought extra concealer, darker foundation to cover the ink blots on my body, but no amount of powder or liquid skin could disguise the pain on my chest, my arms, my thighs. I hated this weak, rag doll costume, despised the way they'd come when I screamed, when I flinched, when I bled, and so the next time they hit me, I hit them back. And some of them never got up.

Harlot

She wasn't usually open to new ideas, to new positions, and new friends, but she wanted to be, so she pretended that she was someone who could handle it, someone who could be with men, who could be with women, who could be with men and women, and she played and she explored, tasted different dishes from different menus, and somewhere between the foreplay and the sex, between the drunk conversations and the self-rolled joints, she realized that this was who she was and that she no longer had to pretend that she liked it, because she did, she *really, really did*.

He Asked Me to Stay

I'll never forget the first time a man made me coffee in the morning. After years of becoming a practiced leaver, it was strange to wake up in bed alone, to wake up with coffee on the night stand, with breakfast cooking in the kitchen. I remember putting on my Jim Morrison t-shirt, remember fumbling to find my glasses, remember tip-toeing into the living room and being met with eggs and bacon, with a good morning kiss, with a *how did you sleep?* And I stood there, stomach growling, hangover throbbing, naked from the waist down and I said *fine* because I didn't understand what was happening, because I figured we were just friends, because no one had ever done this for me before, and when he asked what we were doing that day, I choked on my coffee and he laughed, and I laughed, and then he said sorry, *I'm not done with you yet* and it was that moment that taught me something about love and I wasn't wearing pants.

Hedonist

With a voice like crushed velvet, he seduced her with his words, with the way his tongue rolled over promises that she knew he couldn't keep, but he was a collision worth having, a sin worth making, and every time he touched her, her skin burned with lust. The devil was inside him, and she liked the way he felt, liked the way he moved against her body, the way he whispered in her ear. If he was Hell, then she'd make sure to sell her soul, and so with every kiss, and every moan, every sigh, and every scream, she made sure to say his name, made sure to etch it in her memory, so that when she walked through the inferno in another life, she could scream for him, she could find him, and maybe she could love him in death, just as she did in life..

Heroin Chic

Say no,
no no no
I never listen
it's always
yes yes yes
higher higher higher
I wake up naked
next to you
holes in my arms
bags under my eyes
drunk, hungover
my vagina sore,
my morals gone
you turn to me
say no
no no no
but I never listen
it's always
yes yes yes

Hotel Room

He gave me the key and sent me upstairs, made me repeat the room number so he knew I wouldn't get lost but I was drunk and after I got in that elevator, I didn't know where my room was let alone his. So I just stayed in there, riding the box up and down, down and up, and eventually, he got in and found me there and he laughed and laughed, kissed me hard on the mouth, and took me in his arms. He carried me into a room—whose number I still don't remember—and then he kissed me some more and then it was morning and I was smiling and he was sleeping and when I left I didn't look at the door, but I bet you I could find that room again, bet you I could find it by memory, by instinct alone.

Hunger

Looking at him made her fierce, made her hungry, animalistic; she wanted to destroy him
and in destroying him, rebuild herself. The urge, too great to ignore,
set fire to her blood, her fantasies, and she couldn't stand to look at him
without picturing him naked and tied to her bedposts: Gagged. Erect. Restrained.
She needed it, demanded it.
It had been too long since they'd made love.
Since they'd fucked.
Since they'd fed.
And all of her sex screamed for him, and when she screamed,
she liked to come, and so the hunt for pleasure, for nourishment began.

I Cover the Wall's Mouth

I hold my hand over the wall's mouth so it can't tell our secrets,
so it can't tell the guests the ways we like to get off, how you like to watch me,
how you harden at the taste of my sex. The walls see the way we look
at each other, hungry, like animals, how we feed when the lights turn off,
how we rise starving with the sun.

I cover the wall's mouth with my lips so it can't scream,
so it can't yell when you push me against the wall,
when you drive me from behind, legs spread, arms pinned above my head.
you want my voice, not the voice of the corners of the room that ache
to be used, not the space behind us, envious of the sounds our bodies make.

You cover the wall's mouth with my hair so it can't speak,
my brown locks wrapped tightly in your fists. You want my moans, my wishes,
you want me to ask for it, want me to beg. And with the wall's mouth covered in silence,
I submit only to you.

Indiscreet

I'll promise to behave
if you promise me you won't;
and I swear no one will know
for I'll seal my lips at the tip of your cock
and this will be our little secret.

Infidelity

The first time she was with a married man, he asked her to pretend to be his wife, to role-play what it would be like to trust each other, to be together. And she did, and she hated it. She didn't like pretending she was someone who cared, someone who loved this man and all his shortcomings, both true and false. That took the fun out of it. He was a stranger, and that's how she preferred it: someone random, someone exciting, someone with experience who could show her a thing or two. But he had to put her on some pedestal that she couldn't—and wouldn't—play up to, so she faked her pleasure, put on a good show, and after he left, she masturbated to the man she thought he was and then she tipped herself for good form as she counted up his cash and threw away his bill.

Infiltrate From Within

My mouth is a war zone,
my teeth spit bullets,
my tongues twists lies.

Intimacy

Living and working in the whore house is a type of intimacy in itself, for you're always being watched, and someone or something is always inside of you, whether it's a memory or a person, and that makes it impossible to be alone. In some ways, there's a strange comfort in that, in the sex, in the possession, in the dirty old men, in the filthy women, in the exchange of juices, and the verbal pleas. It all attaches itself to the walls—the sounds, the tastes, the sights, scents, and feels—and if I close my eyes and concentrate, I can see body against body, hit pause, rewind, and play, watch movies during the day, and live them out at night.

Jilted

I left her, it was a her, wasn't it?
on the steps of St. Agnes church
Amelia, that's what I would have named her
her, with the crystal blue eyes
I can hardly remember
but it was cold and I wrapped her in my shawl
I know the homeless woman I stole it from would smile if she knew
but I cry
and so does she,
Amelia,
my baby girl,
I did this for you

Job Title

Doors closed
eyes shut
she lay beneath sheets
waiting
waiting to be chosen
to be made worthy
to be paid
and the longer she waited
the harder it became to stay
to survive
to remind herself
that she,
she with the closed doors
and the eyes that were shut
was, still, in fact,
a woman

Joint Custody

You own me
just as much as I own myself;
my heart, my spirit, my sex, my love,
it's yours for the taking, as is my body.

Juice

I drip for you,
wet, hot,
ready the second
our eyes meet
and my legs are spreading
before you even open
your mouth,
that mouth
that I expect not see for the next
hour, but that I expect to feel,
feel between my legs,
between my breasts,
and when you make your way
up to my mouth,
then it will be my turn
to disappear beneath sheets,
between legs and your turn
to drip, wet,
hot, and ready,
ready for me,
ready for me.

Just Because

Just because I said 'yes'
does not mean that
I'm happy,
that I'm proud of my decision
to let you in,
to take you in,
and just because I said 'yes'
does not mean that
I wasn't thinking *no*

Justifiable

Snow falls in sync with teardrops on my windowsill and I count them as they collect in frozen pools, for he'll be here soon, soon to tell me that I'm wrong, that I'm delusional, that everything that is happening, isn't happening, that I need to accept that I'm merely a hole he fills when he needs to escape, but that he still loves me in that way that is not a way, that can't be a way, our way…

And there is ice on my heart, and it's freezing my blood in crimson shards that weigh down my chest and make it hard to breathe, and when he knocks on my door, I open it because I don't know how to say goodbye, because I don't know how to walk away from something I believed in and so I justify it, accept it, and I feel like a whore, like a possession that is used, and abused, and thrown away, but for those split seconds when he holds me like he loves me, when he looks at me like I'm the only girl in world, it's worth it even if I can't sleep at night, even if I don't know how to feel anything anymore.

Kama Sutra

Take me from the back,
own me from the front,
I want to be blindfolded with your tie
and told when to speak, and while
I don't like to be controlled, there's something
about the exchange of power,
the not knowing if I can trust you, the ever-changing dominance between you and me
that makes me wet, that turns me on,
and when you think you have me, when you think my body is yours,
I will twist you and turn you,
breaking spines,
breaking bones,
breaking promises and hearts,
for my Kama Sutra is a book of pain,
a book of vengeance that was written by my body
after too many nights of being used
after too many drinks and drunken fights,
jealous moments and unjustifiable pain,
and like a black widow,
I will eat you,
but not after I have taken you first.

Keeping Tabs

He thinks that I don't pay attention,
that I don't notice,
maybe even that I don't care,
but every time he comes and every time he goes,
I'm keeping tabs,
I'm taking notes.

There's no cat and mouse game here,
no hide and seek;
I'm a straight shooter,
always have been
I collect my dues
don't take no for an answer,
and if he cheats me—which he will—
he'll find himself begging, pleading, crying,
because I don't play with pussies,
not unless I'm getting paid.

Killing Strangers

We have a rule here, protect your own, and the girls and I follow it down to the bloody hole where we've dumped a dozen or so of our clients, for you can be a stranger, and you can even be strange—and trust me, I've seen strange, I've done strange, and I've been strange—but at some point, there's a line, and I'm the only one who's allowed to bring a knife into my bed, so please, go ahead. Try to hold me down, try to take me against my will. Don't listen to me when I say stop, because I want to see what happens when the girls hear me scream, hear me gag, hear me choke and they'll lay you down sweetheart, but trust me, I'll write you a tab, because everything I do is for profit and whether I'm killing or fucking, I always get paid.

Kinky as a Definition of Him

He was my steady 5:30 p.m. client, at my door, every Monday, with a suitcase full of debauchery that gave me nightmares and made me sore in places that I didn't know I had; he wore a wedding band and called me his wife's name, and it made me want to kill him and then kill myself, but he paid me triple and my own family was starving, so I stayed late to be his doll, to be his spouse, and then every Monday I'd go home to my husband and cry—and every Monday he'd refuse to look at me.

Kitten

I am not a cat,
and I am not your kitten
and just because my pussy is part of my job
does not mean you can refer to me as animal, as feline,
but if you do,
then know that animals by nature
kill their own kind
and I am no different.

Lady Killer

Women are gentle,
ladies are kind,
at least that's what they want you to think,
think that they're matronly, that they're nurturing,
that they'll love you and care for you as if you were their own,
but fantasies are fantasies for a reason
and the more you believe them,
the harder it will be to believe
that they are knives and they are poison,
neglected lovers and scorned wives;
they are death in unfiltered stereotypes
darkness in violet dresses with red lips,
lips stained with blood, with malice
and I know because I tempted one,
tempted one and saw what she could do,
and it was frightening,
and it was marvelous
and I still wear the scars.

Leaving Him for Dead

She told me she didn't want to do it,
but I knew better; I watched how he treated her,
listened to her scream, and once she told me
she'd let him do things to her outside of work so she could
make a full cut, and when I asked what these *things* were,
she'd cry and walk away.

But as I stood there, there with the body,
his eyes weren't just dead, they were *long* dead,
and hers were alive, relaxed,
washed in calmness, in pride, and she was my friend
so I overlooked the wounds in his back and the blood in his mouth,
and I fixed the situation,
took care of it all,
because I'd been in the business longer than her,
and I knew how to make a body disappear,
how to make all the questions,
all the pain
stop
once
and
for all.

Lewd Behavior

The first time I woke up in a bed that was not my own
with a man I did not know,
with a woman beside me,
her hair tangled in mine,
I felt a strangeness in my chest that I couldn't place,
that I didn't understand,
for after years of monogamy, of faithfulness,
of relationships where I was true, where I was loyal,
here I was now, free, free to explore, to experiment,
to say yes, to say no,
to see what I liked and stop what I didn't
and she was there, and she was beautiful
and so I kissed her
and spread my legs for him, took him, and took her,
because I wasn't responsible for anyone but myself,
myself, and the those who found their way into my bed

Lonely Soul

She listens to the clock tick,
watches the hand move,
circle after circle,
each second a lifetime
as the metronome tocks,
back and forth it sways,
a fearless repetition
she knows all too well

She wakes to a cycle
in and out
days into months
a rotation she can't escape
and the ticking gets louder,
the tocking, too fast,
and like Hook she smashes clocks
shatters glass faces
destroys wooden grins
there's no need for reminders
of what's waiting every hour
on the hour
as she spreads her legs
and goes to work

Love Scars

He was asleep and she was awake, awake and ready, her body and mind aflame. *He won't know, he won't even see it coming.* She lifted the sheets and the scent of sweat and sex hit the air. She smiled and bit her lip in that playful way he liked, and she wondered if he'd like the way she looked now: excited, playful, aroused. She wanted him to remember her forever, to lock her away in his memory box, her name always on the tip of his tongue.

Her hair pin lay on the table next to the bed and this was her favorite part of the game, the part where she left her mark and left her job, just another Jezebel running through the brothel chain. She didn't even work here this time and the thrill of taking a client that wasn't hers, to a room that wasn't her own, made her wicked, made her wet. She carved a one next to her name and blew on his thigh to take away the sting. In some ways, he was her first, the first John that she didn't kill and she thought he deserved to know that. And now every time he fucked another girl, he'd remember that she let him live. That he owed her and he'd pay her back someday, someday when she came back to collect.

But for now, all she needed was her name in his flesh.
A signature so she could identify him when she was ready.

Lust Is My Deadly Sin

Bed is where I'm told I'm supposed to be, sprawled out like some harlot, like some cheap whore so men can come and play with me, throw money at me when they're done, done, like it's ever really finished, like the money actually helps—and sometimes, sometimes it does, but the food I buy with it makes me feel like a glutton, and the roof over my head makes me feel like a sloth, and I can't sleep knowing that my body is a train, a vehicle for passengers whether they have a ticket or not—but this, this life is what I know, and it's what I do and what I've always done, and I'm worried that if I stop, that I'll actually miss it, and that I'll hate myself even more.

Madness

Thoughts into stories,
stories into fantasies,
fantasies into back rooms,
strange men, lapsed morals; they're an unfair addiction
created out of pain, for pain,
because feeling anything is pleasure
when you're constantly numb.

Man-eater

I take my men with whiskey,
swallow them
morning,
noon
and night

Masturbation

Sometimes when she touched herself
she pretended to be another person
someone who loved her,
who cared more about the essence of giving pleasure
rather than taking it for themselves;

And

Sometimes when she touched herself,
she thought about the moments when she smiled,
when men were charming as they tried to court her,
even if those moments were composed of carefully woven lies
sung in order to get between her legs;

And

Sometimes when she touched herself,
she thought about how empty she felt,
how broken, how alone, and when she'd orgasm,
she'd cry, because there was never anyone there
to fill her.

May I?

Never assume you can: be polite,
ask questions, pursue with persistence,
but don't be demanding, unless—of course—they're into that,
then call the shots, lay out the plan,
always lead with pleasure
even if you follow it with pain.

Ménage a trois

Threesomes are a game of dominance,
a test of will, of jealously, of intention; the first one to break has feelings,
the second one to break has remorse,
the third is just happy to get fucked,
and therefore, he, or she, is the winner.

Miscarriage

The child twisted inside me
desperate for escape;
It broke its bones,
shed its skin,
used my blood as lubricant
to slide out between my legs;
It/he/she made its/his/her appearance,
silent, static
a premature suicide
a stillborn angel.

Miss Behave

Darling, girl,
don't be shy,
in this room,
there is no need
for modesty
and I won't give you
points on how well you behave;
show me what you want me to do to you,
tell me with your mouth how you want me to act;
you won't be graded on how hard you try,
you'll be graded on how hard I make you come

Naked

Naked is a state of mind,
not a state of body; it's our vulnerability
that strips us in the end.

Natural Born Sinner

I was born for this:
for open legs
for neon signs
for cash paychecks
and sore limbs;
Yes,
God made me a whore,
a mistress in the sheets, and I feel no shame
for doing what I was put on this earth to do,
to make love, to give pleasure, to work in the best way
that I know how: to serve drinks, to light cigars, to spread laughter,
to incite joy, and it's not me that leaves the house in humiliation
feeling dirty and used: it's you, for you were not born for this,
you stumbled about this, guilty, confused, and weak,
whereas I, I was born for this:
for corsets and lace
for illegal activity
for perfumed pillows
and Johns who cry;
Yes,
Mother made me a whore,
a working-class girl, and I feel no shame
for doing what I was put on this earth to do,
to look pretty, to give patience, to work in the best way
that I know how; to love my body, to respect my body,
to excite my body, and it's not me that leaves the house in disgust: it's you.

Never and Me

Change
change is what I did
what I had to do when I knew that what I wanted
was locked inside of never: never-going-to-happen,
never-allowed-to-be, never, never, never;
and it hurt and I cried
shed my morals like a second skin,
took a wrench and dislocated my heart
because never wasn't me
and yet, here never was, staring me in the face,
forcing me to change, to adapt, to *become*,
so I climbed out of my body and settled into someone else,
someone who I didn't like but couldn't, wouldn't refuse,
and I stepped into her beds, her drinks, her drugs; I explored her,
she who was new, who was not me,
not me at all
and everything that I'd already done
seemed impossible, seemed faked, as if I could never do it again,
as if I never did it to begin with,
never, never, never,
and all those feelings didn't matter,
those lies were obsolete;
never became me,
and never felt good,
like a welcomed tragedy that had been fated and pinned to my chest
like a voicemail that was static;
a quiet reminder
to let some things go,
to change
to adapt
to be
never,
never and
me

New Orleans

Jazz filled the room and light dripped off his fingertips
as he set my body on fire, as he sang to me with his hips,
and I don't know if New Orleans felt the rhythm, or if she
saw the colors dance on the ceiling while I screamed, but
each drink tasted like summer and each sigh felt as cold
as the Mississippi draft.

Nobody's Whore

What you didn't know about sleeping with me
was that you slept with me on my terms;
you didn't say the right things, didn't smooth talk
your way into my cunt, no, you didn't charm your way
into my bed, into my ass, into my heart;
I slept with you because I wanted to,
because I felt like it, because I needed the money,
because I like sex, because I'm not ashamed of who I am or what I do;
I slept with you because it was my choice, because I was lonely,
because I'm strong, because I'm confident, because I was bored,
but mostly, I slept with you because I gave myself permission to,
and I'll promise you now, and tomorrow, and every day after,
that I'm nobody's whore but my own.

Nymphomaniac

The answer is,
and always has been,
yes

Obedience

Laugh one more time
and I'll rip out your tongue; this isn't a joke,
not a game I play for fun, so sit still and remain quiet.

Good

Now take off your clothes,
show yourself to me, present yourself as the
sinful girl you were and ask for my forgiveness,
repent, get down on all fours.

Perfect

Lift up your ass more,
I'm going to put this bandana around your face;
bite down on the cloth, try not to gag,
but if you do, it will not matter.

Mmmmh

No matter how much you scream,
I'm not going to stop; you asked for this,
remember that, with every time you opened your legs,
your lips, your cunt to those other girls, those other men,
you asked for this.

Thirteen times
you asked for this

And because I love you,
it's really going to hurt;
I promise you that

Obituary

Every morning
the paper listed the dead,
their names in newspaper ink; the girls and I
would circle the ones we'd been with,
rate their performance one to ten,
recounting memories, reliving good times,
and then we'd kiss their picture wearing our favorite shade of lipstick,
bid them farewell just as we used to tell them hello.

One-Night Stand

The sheets are in the washing machine
    turning, twisting,
      wet, just like our bodies
Sage and vanilla burns on my windowsill
And my bedroom is stained blush and leather

I can hear the shower running
    steam curls from
    under the door
You're singing out of key; it makes me laugh
But it's my favorite song—so I'll let you stay longer

I slip on my robe but I don't tie it shut
    there's nothing to hide,
    you've seen all of me
I put the tea kettle on, wait for it scream
I know I'll never see you again.

Open for Business, Closed for Love

I didn't grow up wanting to work in a brothel; I grew up wanting to be married and have kids, to live in a nice house in the country where I'd write and paint, where I'd raise a family and tend an herb garden. I dreamed about a ring, not a diamond—I could care less about a diamond—that I would look at every day knowing that someone loved me enough, enough that they wanted me and no one else. I thought about it, prayed about it, begged God for it every day, but God doesn't listen to girls who are attracted to darkness; The Madam does.

I tried hard, was given the chance once, maybe twice, but it was a half chance, an empty chance, and I couldn't lessen myself for love, so I lessened myself for hate, for resentment, for sadness and pain. I crawled into the gutter and slept with a needle in my arm. I sprinted to the back alley and drank a paper bag full of poison. The slit between my legs grew hungry, hungry for anything other than rejection, so I turned tricks so I could feel whole, so I could feel wanted, maybe even loved.

The brothel wasn't my first choice, but it was the best choice for who he left me to be. The whore house saved me, took me in like a father, like a mother, like a husband, like a wife, and when the Madam slipped her ring on my finger, who was I to say no?

Orgasm

The French refer to the orgasm as "the little death,"
la petite mort, and the ladies and I laugh every time
we fuck, every time we get paid,
because our paychecks came from
the men with dirty secrets
that we buried
sex feet deep
beneath the
house
after giving them
one last night
of pleasure,
one last reason
to smile.

Out of Service Sign

This is ~~not~~ a brothel.
Please~~, do not~~ come in.

Peepshow

Love is a performance,
an act worth watching; if you give her a piece of silver,
she'll show you what she can do with her mouth; if you give her a piece of gold,
she'll show you what she can do, all she can do, but be mindful: look, do not touch,
for men have lost more than hands that way.

Penance

Every time he left, I went into the bathroom and scrubbed my flesh raw, taking shower after shower until I couldn't feel him anymore. Often, I would I stand there, let the boiling water burn my skin, and sometimes, I would sit beneath the spray and cry, cry knowing that my tears were pointless, that no one, not even myself could discern them from the droplets that singed my cheeks in fresh baptism, telling me to pray, to renew myself, my body, through the isolated fire until I blistered, until I broke. Only then would I be forgiven. Only then would I be pure.

Perversion

Tongues twist and slide against one another,
drinking, slurping,
tasting the juice of attraction, of seduction;
everything is wet and everything is ripe,
and she wonders if the rest of him is sweet,
if his flavor will sit well on her palate when she takes him in;
hands fumble, finding curves, exploring crevices,
moving, inserting,
touching the elixir, fingering the sap;
she salivates and swallows—
everything is wet, everything is ripe,
and he tastes like summer in her mouth.

Photograph

Still shot,
bent over,
my stilettos scrape your floor;

Take me in black and white,
in a lace garter;
my thigh-highs velvet against
your film;

Frame by frame,
twist me, turn me,
position after position,
make me into art.

Pillow Fight

A white duvet against milky flesh,
two goose-feather pillows, one underneath my head,
one underneath his, and there is peace in the color,
in the stillness, in the quiet; I breathe a sigh of relief,
my hands no longer shaking, his chest no longer rising.

Purge

There's food inside of me
it sticks to my hips, my stomach, my thighs,
fat fat fat
I don't want you to see me
not like this
not with this ugliness stuck to my bones,
puffing up my face,
swelling my breasts;
get it out of me,
cancel out the calories,
delete the one-too-many meals
let's fuck till I can't breathe
till I'm sore and sweating,
exercise me till I'm weak,
choke me till I vomit,
it all makes me feel beautiful
makes me feel thin
erased,
half of who I am
the only half that anyone ever cares
to see

Queen of Hearts

She carried a cage made of bone to each room she visited and placed it on the bedside table. It watched her as she worked, as she fed with her tongue, slurping, slapping, flicking in and out and when the time came—*when they came*—the cage stretched its porcelain legs, sulked over on ivory spikes and buried itself into their chests. Calcium claws ripped out hearts filled with adrenaline, juiced up with sex, and then it ate them out just as its mistress did, neither of them leaving anything behind.

Queer

This business isn't about labels;
no one here is straight, gay, or bi—
but I'm willing to be that after you've had a taste of both,
the word queer will be offensive
because pleasure is pleasure
once you've spread your legs
and opened your mind a bit.

Quickie

Around noon we get a slight bump in business; men, women, men/women from all around town come to us on their lunch breaks, come to us in fifteen minutes or less, and it's quick, and it's fast, and it's the easiest way to make twenty dollars while you lie down and plan what you're making for dinner that night.

Quiet, They're on to Us

The last room on the right is known as the *Reflection Room*. It's protocol to go there after seeing clients so the girls can think about what they did and how they did it. There's a journal on the table, some write in it, some don't, but the ones who do are angry and most of the scribbles don't make sense. The pages are wet with tears, and none of them want to do it, but they have to do it, and this game we all play is just as mental as it is physical, and if blokes keep disappearing, the pigs are eventually going to show up,

so the girls need to be practiced,
need to be quiet,
need to know how to stay composed
while others decompose,
need to learn to talk
without saying a word

Quitting Time

After the last Jane left,
I stripped the bed and took a shower—a cold shower—
because it's hard to turn off
after you've spent the whole day on.

Remember Not to Cry

It was a strange feeling to be both alive and dead,
and no matter how much I smoked, drank, or fucked,
I couldn't decide which hell was worse:
I knew that whatever I was doing wasn't working,
and that's why I continued to do it.

Replacement

There are lines and folds on my body that weren't there a year ago. Men pass me over in favor of younger, riper women, and I sit in my room, the draft cold against my naked flesh, waiting, watching, wondering if I still have it—the ability to seduce, to attract. I used to just make eye contact with a man, and he'd follow me to dark corners, to empty rooms, but they don't see me anymore and now my tits sag and my legs aren't as strong.

It's hard to admit it here, on this bed, the bed where I've had countless men and countless women, that I've lost it—the ability to seduce, to attract. That I'm dried up. Tired. Worn. I bleed when I shouldn't, I crack when I move, and this bed, this house, deserves someone better, someone strong. It deserves a Madam who can fuck it back when it's fucking her.

Resilient

This job isn't a clock in, clock out kind of gig. Sure, I have my days when I'm expected to show up, but even after the house *closes*, I still remain open, open to back alleys, bar bathrooms, parked cars and wooden benches. I sleep when I can, eat when the hunger's too much to ignore, but this life is *go, go, go,*

and a girl has to be available,
has to be able to bounce back
has to always be ready and willing
for more.

Ripped Stockings

Holes make a star appearance on vulgarized flesh,
as my attempt to be ladylike fails;
there's a rip near my crotch
and it does nothing
but make me
laugh

Rough Play

The door wasn't shut all the way,
and my curiosity was wide open. There were two sets of hands
with ropes fashioned around their wrists, the knots tied like jewelry
to accent the bit someone had stuffed into their mouths. I couldn't catch their eyes
but they didn't seem to be hurt;
they seemed to be enjoying it,
their sighs, moans, and gentle gaps
like wasp wings in the air.

Route 70 at Midnight

I felt my heart more than usual that night
I gripped the steering wheel a little tighter
drank a little quicker
and all the cigarettes in my glove compartment were gone
and I hadn't heard from him in days.

I watched the lines on the highway start to blur
I pulled off to the side of the road
threw my beer bottle against a tree
and I could no longer write to the sound of my tears
and I hadn't seen him in weeks.

I shook as the tractor trailers screamed my name
I sat down on the guardrail
on the cold side of alone
and all the worries in my head were true
and I hadn't said his name in months.

Sadism

I don't believe in violence, but after all the abuse—the bruises, the blood, the broken bones—it's nice to play the part every once in a while, to grab his throat, to push him down, tell him what to do, when to do it, how I want it. He might not have taught me anything about love, but he taught me a lot about sex.

It's all about control.

Secret Lovers

Whisper
They can't know that we're together
Take me against the wall
Hide me under the covers
You think I like this?
I do
The wrongness of it
Turns me on
Makes me wet
Makes me come
Hard
Hard
Hard
Be quiet
They'll hear us
They'll know that we're in love
We don't even know that
We pretend
We hide, we play
We walk away
Just make sure no one sees us
No can know but us
Because then we can still deny it
Then we don't have to admit
That
We're
Not a secret
Anymore,
Not even to each other

Sexual Scars

There are scars on my lips
from where you kissed me goodbye;
I touch them in the morning when I look in the mirror;
sometimes they bleed little crimson drops,
double half-ovals that look like hearts,
and it's strange to think you put them there,
that you cut me open and filled me with memories of leaving,
left me chapped and scabbed,
my mouth a solemn gravesite that still echoes your taste.

Shameless Sex
For Kristina

The Madam told me to put on a fresh pair of underwear every morning, and at the end of the day, I was to masturbate in them, to really let myself go. When I was finished, she instructed me to put them in a plastic bag and place them outside her bedroom door. The next morning, the bag would be gone and in its place would be fifteen dollars; a crisp ten and five, once a day, every day, seven days a week.

Slippery When Wet

Wet
Wet
Wet
Make it slide
Make it stick;
Let me see it run down your thigh,
Down your leg,
Down your calf,
Blood
Blood
Blood
Make it slide
Make it stick;
Let me see it run out your mouth,
Down your chin,
Down your throat,
Die
Die
Die
Make it slide
Make it stick;
Let me see it in your eyes,
In your stare
In your face
Sex
Sex
Sex
Make it slide
Make it stick;
Let me touch myself in peace
In your memory
In my room

Stripped

Clothes littered the ground: my bra, my underwear, my t-shirt. I kissed him with nothing on, not even my pride. There was no part of me that wanted to be there, but pleasure was something that I was good at; I liked to give it, and I didn't mind receiving it, but no part of this was for the sex or for the money. Stripping my morals allowed me to become numb, to become unfeeling,

sociopathic,
emotionless.

Nothing hurt anymore. If they didn't call, it was hardly a loss; if I never saw them again, I didn't mind. Sex was a way to fill my time and not be alone, a way to stave off the encroaching darkness that slipped between my sheets at night if I was the only person in my bed. I didn't cry when someone lay next to me, and sometimes, I pretended

that I even
wanted to live.

Symmetry

Girls fit together
when they attach at the waist
and yet some people
still think it's
wrong

The Shed

He sang karaoke while two guys fought
They knocked over a table
We got free drinks
There was a lot of Jameson
There was a shot that tasted like a rotten apple
Maybe it was a rotten apple?
I didn't care
I drank one
I drank two
I drank one. too. many.
He tugged on my jacket,
Kissed the whiskey off my lips
It was time to leave
We danced out the bar
We danced into the rain
And everything was wet
I was wet
Wet
Wet
Wet
And there was a shed on display across the parking lot
It was open
An invitation
We didn't have to discuss it
We never had to discuss it
He put me against the wall
I pulled down my skirt
He pulled up my shirt
Were people watching?
Did I care?
He was inside me
It felt good

And we laughed
Laughed a lot
Because that's what we did
Because we were in a shed
Because we were actually *fucking* in a shed
And we were drunk
Well, I was drunk,
And I kept thinking
If you have sex, you die
Because that's what happens in horror movies
Because the irony was too much
Because I came then,
Came hard, and came laughing,
Thinking about horror, thinking about sheds
Thinking about his dick slapping against my clit,
About how his body was pressed against mine,
About how his body fit inside mine,
About how our sex smelled like rain
Like spring
Like summer
And how when we'd leave
We'd still be wet
Wet
Wet
Wet
But not
From the
Rain

Tied and Taken

Blindfolded
Gagged
Hands tied behind my back—
I tried to control my breathing,
One, two,
In, out,
Claustrophobia
Panic
It never used to bother me,
Not until the one time I couldn't escape,
Couldn't escape the beatings, the abuse
Crying
Whispered screams
I don't want to be here
It hurts to remember
The blindfold only makes me see,
See it all again
I relive it
Blindfolded
Gagged
Hands tied behind back—
He gives me fifty dollars
I cut my wrists

Tipsy, Tanked, Trashed

My tongue is accustomed to burning, my palate, to pain,
because every time I ask to be fucked,
he always says yes;
It takes little to no time
before he's in my mouth, before he's coming down my throat,
coming in waves of whiskey,
in oceans of bourbon, in seas of gin;
sometimes it catches and I wince,
shake the tears from my eyes,
wipe the spittle from my chin,
but I know what I asked for,
and I know he can provide,
Drink Drink Drink
Swallow Swallow Swallow
I don't want to remember
and the bottle helps me to forget

Transaction

I
am
Nothing
but a business transaction,
something—not someone—
and you do me without feeling, without concern, for
I
am
Nothing
but a job,
something—not someone—
you use for convenience, always discreet,
fearing not to hide me
behind shadows, behind closed doors, for
I
am
Nothing,
but a window-shopped memory,
something—not someone—
that you forget the second you leave, and,
You
are
Everything
someone—not something—
to me, me who waits
in bed, at home, at work,
praying that someday, I won't be
Nothing
to
You

Trust Me

Trust me,
I do this all the time;
there's nothing to be afraid of,
nothing
except me.

The Flavor

I wake up with it in my mouth,
it sits on my tongue,
that acrid, sweet flavor,
that bitter, soft tang;
I smile, lick my lips
light comes in through my bedroom window
fills the room,
saturates my face
and everything is red
and everything is blood

Ugly Little Moment

Blood-stained
Sex-crazed
She was just a girl
When they took her
When they ate her
When they fucked her

She didn't like it
Didn't want it
Bit back,
Teeth through flesh
Tonguing blood
Chewing bone

She tried to stop
Couldn't help it
Couldn't fight it

Blood-stained
Sex-crazed
She was just a girl
When she took them
When she ate them
When she fucked them dead

Unanimous

Yes:
that's the magic word
but neither of us had to say it—
it was obvious
what needed to be done,
and my mouth was too busy
to speak

Untamed

She
smiled
a gone,
a gone like cigarette smoke
like the last sip in the bottle,
like the first ten minutes into a good high;
free and wild,
she took to the sun, danced to the moon
an effervescent spirt,
a child of gypsies, of wanderers—
she made money when she had to,
when she wanted to,
always on the run,
never with a destination;
free—
free like air,
like river water
like daisies in the summer
and no one owned her,
not even if they bought her
because body is not soul
and soul is
what she was
and what she was
was
gone—
gone,
girl,
gone.

Untie Me

Bound in heart,
Tongue-tied and confined
There's no movement in this house
I'm stagnant,
Motionless,
You make me quiet,
Still.

Untie me,
Cut off the rope,
Take off the shackles
It hurts too much to be here
Trapped,
Directionless,
You have me crying,
Begging.

Release me,
Tell me you're sorry,
Whisper that I'm free
Love is an entrapment,
A setup,
And you have me secured,
Knotted to your heart

Used

There is a phone call
There is a fifteen minute drive
There is a knock at the door
There is a hello
There is a touch
There is a fuck
There is a goodbye

There are no feelings
There are no thoughts
There are no decisions
There are no concerns

There is only passion
There is only pain
There is only regret

Regret
Regret
Regret

Vaginal Roses

She opens like a flower,
blossoms summer,
rains a delicate spring;
once a month, she bleeds roses,
births red petals for days,
for 12 weeks out of the year;
like Georgia O'Keefe paintings
she paints her body with botany,
bloodies her canvas
with crimson paint that
fills gardens
and plants eggs,
death to life
with sweet
feminine blood.

Velvet Underground

Soft girl
Sweet girl
Purr for me,
P u r r r r r r r

My good girl
My velvet girl
Now open for me
A h h h h h h h h

Scream girl
Yell girl
Fly for me
F l y y y y y

Vibrate

Body on,
Shaking,
Trembling,
He's inside
Me
He's part of
Me
I ache
He cries
I come
He sighs

Vicious Girls

Creatures,
creatures are what they are—
violent Eves, rotten apples,
victimized damsels, Salem witches;
they bit the snake that fed them
drank his poison,
pulled out his fangs
and now they bleed,
they bleed once a month for his death,
the death of the devil who cursed their wombs
for they are vicious,
they are venomous
they are women,
and they will wait,
patient and persistent,
ever-enduring
and damned
and they will sing,
sing in covens, sing in brothels,
sing for men,
sing for whores
and their words will kill
they will damn
they will puncture
for they sing with lips,
lips not of mouth but of sex
sex that weakens, that confuses,
that traps
and once they have you
have you between their legs,

they will kill you,
they will eat you,
and they will love you
the only way
that they know how

Violent Fantasies

No tattoos,
Just cuts, incisions:
One,
Two,
Three plus more,
Down my side
Across my stomach;
I punish my body
For every man I've fucked,
Every girl I've broken
Every heart I've destroyed.

Viper Bite

You come on my face
slithering, writhing;
like a snake you bite my flesh,
inject me with your seed
and like that,
I am bitten,
I am smitten
I am yours.

Waltz

The first time he kissed me it was unexpected and it was spontaneous and we were in my car, my car that I just bought and I remember him saying "I'm sorry but I just have to do this" and I remember laughing, laughing into his kiss, his tongue moving against mine, dancing in my mouth. We stayed there for a long time, waltzing in the car, spinning and turning with our mouths and now I remember that kiss, that man, that love, every time I dance, every time I sing.

Watching Him

He fucked her while I watched,
while I sat there in the corner,
while I smoked my last cigarette,
one hand between my legs;
he found me
when he got close,
his back arched
his breath ragged,
our stares connected
as she came,
as we came,
as my cigarette
went
out

Weaning Myself Off

Love is a whore's game—
You have to give a part of yourself away in order to get something back and
Sometimes you do and sometimes you don't,
Most times you don't,
But I still sold myself over and over,
Again and again,
Always to him,
Him and no one else,
My body, my spirit, my soul,
I had to stop
Had to stop the trying, the begging, the pleading
I wasn't his girl,
Wouldn't be his girl
And at some point,
The sex became too painful
A loveless pleasure
Between bodies absent of heart,
An exchange of passion
Void of reality,
Of truth,
And of faith.

Welcome

Take your jacket off,
stay a while,
this is a place of play, of pleasure;
touch whatever, *whoever* you like,
just be mindful that each hole is a different price,
and nothing and no one you do here is free.

Whipping Post

Leather—
the sight of it,
the smell of it,
the touch of it,
I want it on your skin,
against your skin,
skin that's red
that's whipped,
that's tender

Don't speak—
stare at the ground
stare at my boots
boots that are leather,
that are black
that are shined

My heel is in your back—
it's sharp
there's blood
you moan
you scream
I whip you again
and again
and again

White Dahlia Abortion

She was with child
I knew about it
so did he,
I'm guessing that's why he killed her,
security, family
a bastard fathering a bastard
a dent in his perfect life
a dirty little secret;

He left the child in her,
wrapped in death
suffocating on its own blood
but I saved him—
I took him out
tore him from his coffin-womb
bathed his blue skin
clothed his precious stone face;

I loved her
my girl with the glassed-over eyes,
with the red smile sewn into her neck;
she was my lover, my friend, my partner
and her child was mine,
mine to protect, to foster, to save,
just like she was,
just like she is,
and the air conditioner is on
buzzing, humming, keeping them cool,
preserved, fresh;

I'll keep them both with me now,
never out of my sight
never far from my reach
my White Dahlia girl
my porcelain baby boy

Wordplay

We sat down and wrote together,
wrote stories and wrote poems,
sometimes we'd write music, me on piano
him on guitar, and we'd sing and we'd recite
sharing scars, bandaging wounds, and it hurt but it felt good and
at some point, our hands stopped making art,
our mouths silent with no more words as they found other uses,
other vices, and we were passionate, in lust, entranced,
and so poetically in love with the idea of each other
that it was too late to learn from the truth
in the stories that we told
every time we cried.

X-rated

I don't come with a warning label,
but I promise that my show
is for adults only.

Xenophile

Don't tell me your name
Don't show me your heart
The last thing I want to do is get to know you—
Knowing people, men, women, it complicates matters,
Makes them painful,
Makes them sting,
I don't want to be heartbroken,
Don't want to have to heal
I want to be strange with strangers
Turned on and aflame with nothing on my mind but sex
Sex
Sex
Sex
So don't say a word
Don't tell me your dreams
Don't tell me your past
I don't want to fall in love with you
I just want to fuck
I just want to feel
Feel something,
Anything,
Anything other than love

Yawn

He spent hours down there,
there, where I was supposed to shower
where I was supposed to be spring,
but no matter how hard he tried
he couldn't make me rain.

Yell for Help

She carried a suitcase
Set it on the bureau
I never asked her what was inside of it
And she never told me,
Not until that night, that night she came in
Pushed me on the bed
Duct-taped my mouth shut
Told me to scream

When I tried, she hit me,
Hit me hard,
Not with an open hand
But with a fist
I could taste my bruises
Feel the blood pumping out my lips

I was scared, humiliated
I started to cry
She duct-taped my eyes
And all I could see
Was darkness
Darkness while she fucked me
Fucked me with something sharp
Something that made me bleed

She carried a suitcase
Set it on the bureau
I never asked her what was inside of it
But part of me always knew

Yellow Dress

I
wore
a
yellow
dress
the first time I met him;
it accented my hair, made the blush in my cheeks
look sweet against innocent eyes,
eyes that lied the moment
they saw him
for
I
wore
a
yellow
dress
to look the part;
to look childish, kind,
when I was neither of these things,
for I was wicked
and I was working
but you'd never guess,
not with me,
not
in
my
little
yellow
dress

Yes-Girl

She didn't know how to say no
How to say it hurt
How to say *stop*...

You, Always You
For You

I close my eyes
remember him lighting candles,
remember him telling me to stay dressed
that he wanted the privilege of unwrapping me
piece
by
piece. I remember his blue bandana,
his long brown hair,
him holding me,
kissing me, telling me
this was how love was supposed to be made
not fast,
not hurried,
but soft.

YouTerUs

You
are inside me,
me/ me and you
and you tear us,
you hurt, you claw,
you rip your way out
I bleed/ bleed strong
bleed red
it hurts, but you come,
you breathe
you tear us/
tear me
in half.

Zelophilia

Her vagina is a hunter
feeding on jealously,
envious rage;
her jaws won't open
unless she's provoked

About the Author

Stephanie M. Wytovich is an instructor of English by day and a horror writer by night. She is the poetry editor for Raw Dog Screaming Press, a book reviewer for *Nameless Magazine*, and the assistant to Carlow University's international MFA program for Creative Writing. She is a member of the Science Fiction Poetry Association, an active member of the Horror Writers Association, and a graduate of Seton Hill University's MFA program for Writing Popular Fiction. Her Bram Stoker Award-nominated poetry collections, *Hysteria: A Collection of Madness*, *Mourning Jewelry*, *An Exorcism of Angels*, and *Brothel* can be found at www.rawdogscreaming.com, and her debut novel, *The Eighth*, will be out in 2016 from Dark Regions Press. Follow Wytovich at stephaniewytovich.blogspot.com and on twitter @JustAfterSunset